WEIRD AND
WONDERFUL
AIRCRAFT

Published 1975 by Enterprise Books
Secausus, New Jersey

Copyright © 1975 by Intercontinental Book Productions
Library of Congress Catalog Card Number 74—24829

ISBN 0—89009—032—7

Printed and bound in Belgium

WEIRD AND WONDERFUL
AIRCRAFT

Written by Graeme Cook
Illustrated by John Wood and Associates
Cover illustration Brian Edwards

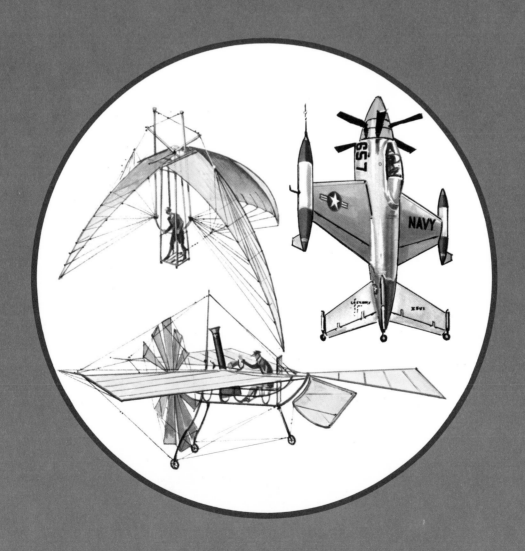

ENTERPRISE BOOKS

Contents

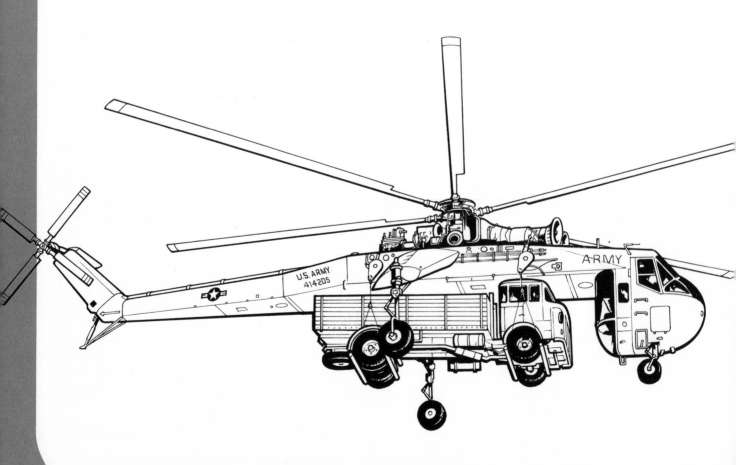

Introduction

Man's conquest of the air has, over the centuries, tested the inventive skill of aircraft designers and builders throughout the world. Until that momentous day in 1903 when two American brothers, Orville and Wilbur Wright, made the first ever sustained, powered and controlled flight, success had eluded those who sought to conquer the skies in an airplane.

Inventors, many of whom were regarded as 'crack-pots,' worked in garden sheds and back-rooms, dreaming up new ideas, designing and building their 'flying' machines. But although some of them reached the threshold of a breakthrough, real success escaped them.

Today these early designs, and indeed many of the flying machines that came after them, look almost comic. But weird as they may seem, without them there would be no *Concorde*, no faster-than-sound jet or swing-wing fighter.

From this evolution in flight have come some truly weird and wonderful airplanes, and the story of these splendid machines and the men who flew them fills the pages of this book.

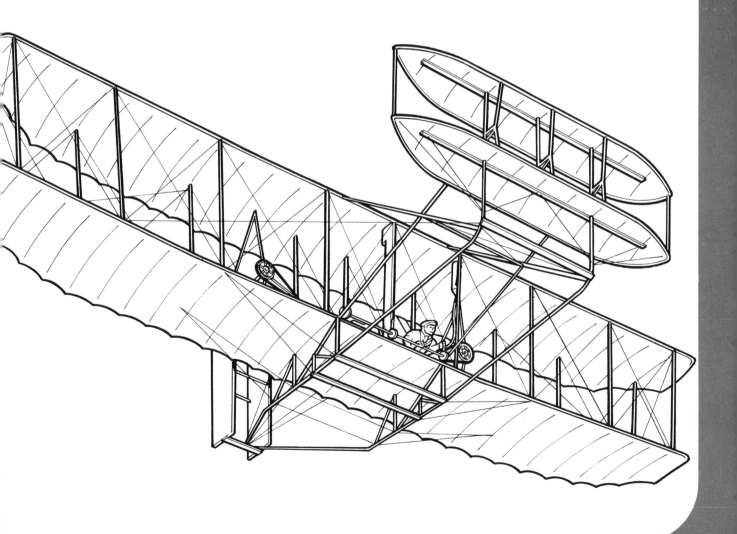

Balloons & Airships

The first aircraft ever to rise into the air did so vertically. It was a hot-air balloon, the brain-child of two French brothers, Joseph and Etienne Montgolfier. Quite by accident, while sitting at home by the fire, they noticed small pieces of paper floating upwards into the chimney. One of them remarked upon this and they reasoned that if the heat of the fire could lift these small pieces, then greater heat would lift larger pieces.

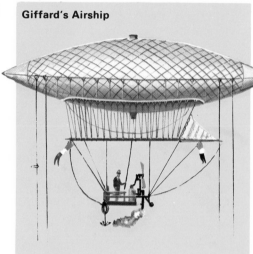

Giffard's Airship

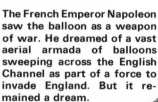

Montgolfier's Hot-Air Balloon

Two Frenchmen, Joseph and Etienne Montgolfier, designed this hot-air balloon, the first to fly with living creatures on board. On September 19, 1783, it rose before an astonished crowd in Paris. Its passengers — a sheep, a rooster and a duck.

The first airship to fly. Powered by a 3-hp steam engine, it was designed and flown by Frenchman Henri Giffard in 1852. It reached a top speed of 6 mph and made a memorable flight from Paris to Trappes, but was found to lack controllability.

The French Emperor Napoleon saw the balloon as a weapon of war. He dreamed of a vast aerial armada of balloons sweeping across the English Channel as part of a force to invade England. But it remained a dream.

The Montgolfier brothers experimented with a small silk bag which shot to the ceiling when placed over the heat. Then they made tests on a grander scale.

On June 5, 1783, they proved their theory by sending aloft a huge balloon 38 feet in diameter and filled with hot air. In September, they advanced still further by flying a larger balloon, carrying the first creatures ever to fly — a sheep, a rooster and a duck. The experiment was a complete success.

In October, a young French doctor became the first man to fly when he rose into the air in the *Montgolfier*, another of the brothers' balloons.

'Napoleon's' Balloon

The floodgates opened and other ballooners took to the air. A succession of strange but successful designs followed. When the Prussians laid siege to Paris in 1870, it was balloons which ferried people and mail out of the encircled city.

But the balloons had one serious drawback; they were at the mercy of the wind, and a pilot had little or no control over his craft. It was clear that some means or form of power unit was needed to control its flight.

The answer was found by another Frenchman, Henri Giffard, when in 1852 he built his airship, an enormous gas bag with a 'gondola' suspended beneath it. To the gondola he attached a 3-hp steam engine which powered a propeller, but, even so, Giffard found his airship difficult to control in flight, although he made an epic trip in it.

There followed other designs, including both clockwork and electrically-

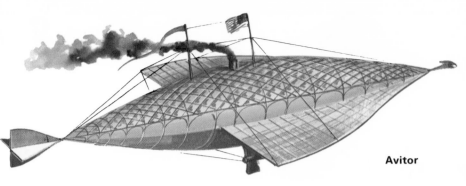

Avitor

Zeppelins were used as bombers in the First World War, then later fitted out with palatial rooms to become passenger airships. But the gas used inside them was highly inflammable, and a series of terrible accidents brought the era of the airship to an end.

On July 2, 1869, American designer Frederick Mariott demonstrated a model of his Avitor steam-driven airship. Shaped like a cigar, it was 37 feet long and 11 feet wide at the middle. Although it flew successfully in a large hall, it came to grief when tested outside in the wind.

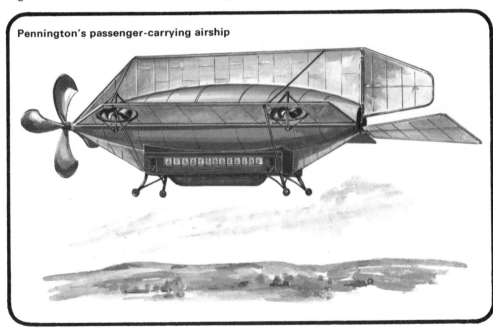

Pennington's passenger-carrying airship

American inventor E. J. Pennington drew up designs for this passenger-carrying airship. Forward movement was to be achieved by the large vertical propeller at the nose, while smaller horizontal fans provided lifting and descending power. It is unlikely that it was ever built.

Santos Dumont, a Brazilian, was the first man to marry the gasoline engine to the airship, and in 1901 he won a 125,000 franc prize when he flew this airship from Saint-Cloud, round the Eiffel Tower in Paris, and back again in less than 30 minutes.

powered balloons, but the real turning point came in 1898 when the Brazilian Santos Dumont fitted a gasoline engine in his airship. His craft was non-rigid, that is it relied upon the gas inside it to maintain its shape.

Then came the most lasting of all the true airships, the German Zeppelin, designed by Count Ferdinand von Zeppelin. His machine had a rigid framework, inside which was a series of hollow compartments filled with gas. The entire airship was then covered with fabric. The gas gave the airship its lift, while engines in the gondolas beneath it provided the forward power.

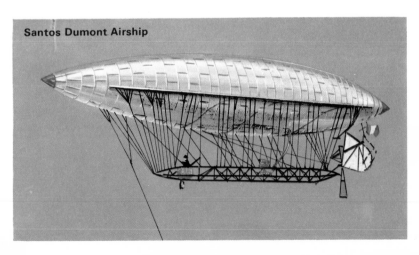

Santos Dumont Airship

Gliders

In 1709, a Jesuit priest, Laurenco de Gusmao, designed the *Passarola* (great bird) and built it as a model. Although somewhat crude and comic in appearance, this weird craft is thought to have flown.

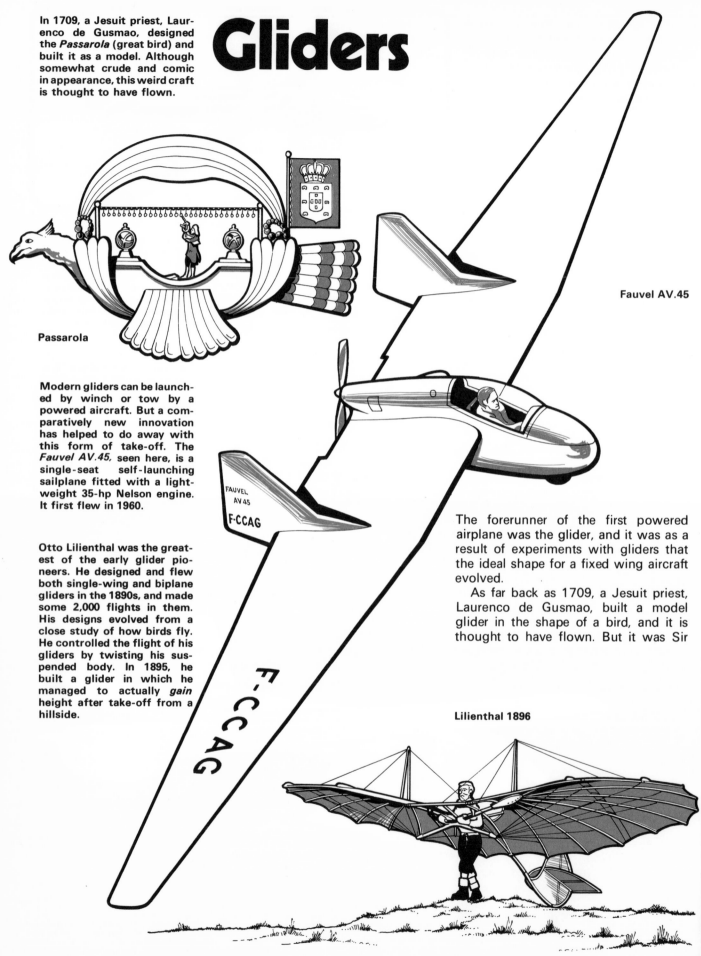

Passarola

Fauvel AV.45

Modern gliders can be launched by winch or tow by a powered aircraft. But a comparatively new innovation has helped to do away with this form of take-off. The *Fauvel AV.45,* seen here, is a single-seat self-launching sailplane fitted with a lightweight 35-hp Nelson engine. It first flew in 1960.

Otto Lilienthal was the greatest of the early glider pioneers. He designed and flew both single-wing and biplane gliders in the 1890s, and made some 2,000 flights in them. His designs evolved from a close study of how birds fly. He controlled the flight of his gliders by twisting his suspended body. In 1895, he built a glider in which he managed to actually *gain* height after take-off from a hillside.

The forerunner of the first powered airplane was the glider, and it was as a result of experiments with gliders that the ideal shape for a fixed wing aircraft evolved.

As far back as 1709, a Jesuit priest, Laurenco de Gusmao, built a model glider in the shape of a bird, and it is thought to have flown. But it was Sir

Lilienthal 1896

FAUVEL AV 45

F·CCAG

F-CCAG

George Cayley, the British aircraft designer, who built and flew the first successful model glider.

Cayley's glider consisted of a long pole with a wing mounted on it and a moveable cruciform tail. In 1853, he built a full-size version with modifications and improvements. Not wishing to risk his own life, he 'persuaded' his coachman to fly it across a valley on his estate. The flight was a success and the coachman became the first man to fly in a heavier-than-air craft. But he was so terrified by his experience that he immediately resigned from Cayley's service.

Inspired by Cayley's success, a German, Otto Lilienthal, built a series of gliders and carried out more than 2,000 flights in them. He, more than any other, made a significant contribution to flying development, for he kept detailed notes of his experiments which were of great value to those who followed.

Lilienthal risked his life every time he took to the air, and fate finally caught up with him when, in 1896, he fell to his death from one of his gliders as it soared down a hillside.

Following in his footsteps, the English flying enthusiast Percy Pilcher and the American Octave Chanute built and flew gliders based on Lilienthal's designs.

Two American brothers, Orville and Wilbur Wright, were fascinated by the achievements of these men, and it was as a direct result of this that, in 1903, they succeeded in making the first ever powered, heavier-than-air, controlled flight.

The advent of the powered aircraft by no means halted the advance in glider design, and gliding became popular as a sport, so much so that it has now grown into a world-wide activity.

With Man's superior knowledge of aerodynamics, the glider has become a brilliant piece of airplane design.

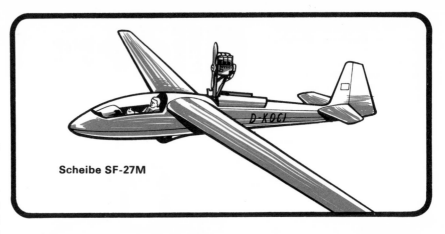

Scheibe SF-27M

The *Scheibe SF-27M* single-engined powered sailplane, which first flew in the 1960s, has a retractable engine. Once airborne, the engine is manually tucked away in its housing behind the cockpit when the pilot wishes to soar.

The *Takatori SH-8 Glider* is a Japanese-built two-seat water-borne sailplane. It is one of the most up-to-date gliders and first flew in 1970. It can take off by being towed into the air by a powerboat and can land on water. It has achieved speeds of up to 112 mph.

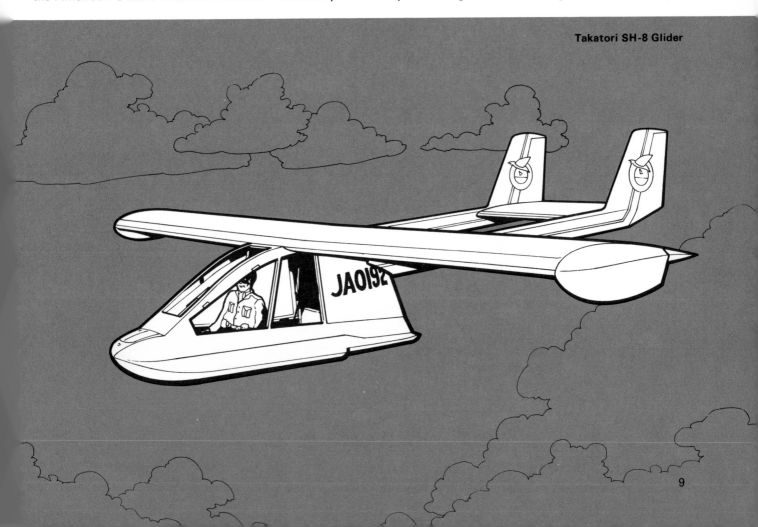

Takatori SH-8 Glider

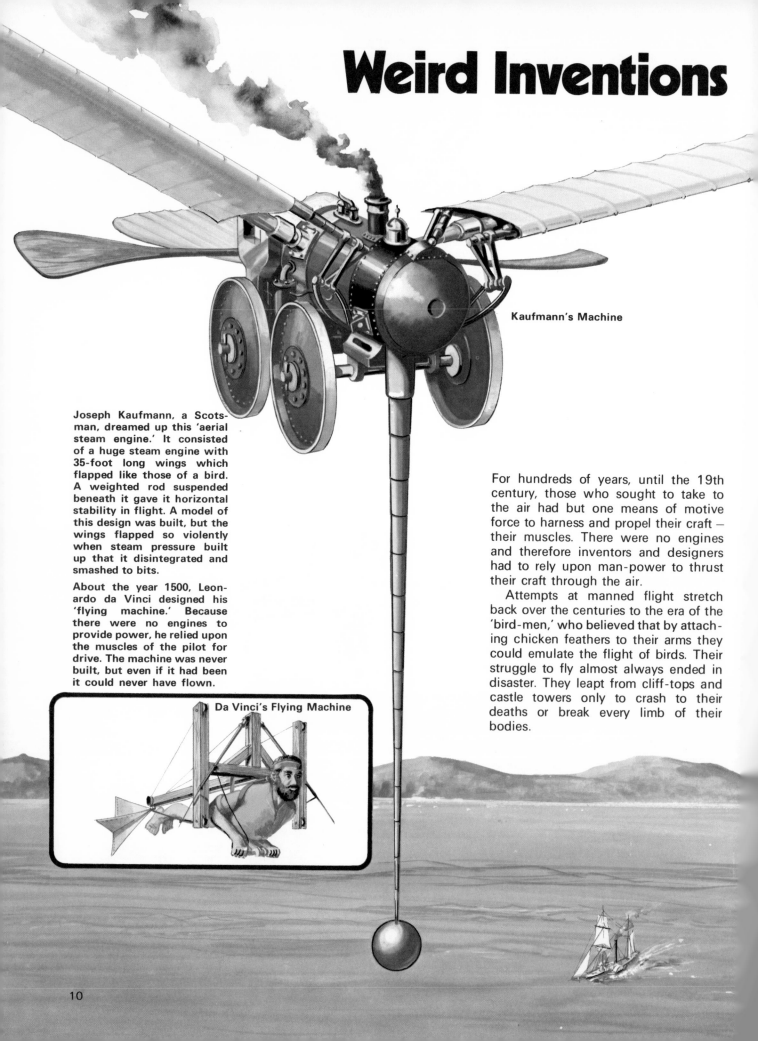

Weird Inventions

Kaufmann's Machine

Joseph Kaufmann, a Scotsman, dreamed up this 'aerial steam engine.' It consisted of a huge steam engine with 35-foot long wings which flapped like those of a bird. A weighted rod suspended beneath it gave it horizontal stability in flight. A model of this design was built, but the wings flapped so violently when steam pressure built up that it disintegrated and smashed to bits.

About the year 1500, Leonardo da Vinci designed his 'flying machine.' Because there were no engines to provide power, he relied upon the muscles of the pilot for drive. The machine was never built, but even if it had been it could never have flown.

For hundreds of years, until the 19th century, those who sought to take to the air had but one means of motive force to harness and propel their craft — their muscles. There were no engines and therefore inventors and designers had to rely upon man-power to thrust their craft through the air.

Attempts at manned flight stretch back over the centuries to the era of the 'bird-men,' who believed that by attaching chicken feathers to their arms they could emulate the flight of birds. Their struggle to fly almost always ended in disaster. They leapt from cliff-tops and castle towers only to crash to their deaths or break every limb of their bodies.

Da Vinci's Flying Machine

More enlightened men, like Leonardo da Vinci, attempted to design machines which could fly, but the lack of proper power units defeated their attempts.

Joseph Degan, another would-be aviator, claimed to have built a flapping wing machine which lifted him a few feet off the ground. But this could hardly be hailed as a breakthrough in 'powered' flight, for he attached a balloon to his contraption.

Throughout the years there continued to be isolated attempts at flight, but it was not until the latter half of the 19th century that an era of airplane invention began which gripped inventors in Europe and America. The race to become the first man to build and fly a heavier-than-air powered airplane was on.

Men like Sir George Cayley, Otto Lilienthal, Percy Pilcher and Octave Chanute had already made dramatic strides in glider design. Balloons had given man his first taste of flying, but there was still a longing to achieve powered and controlled flight and inventors in many lands stretched their imaginations to reach this. In garden sheds, disused barns, back-rooms, and many of the most unlikely places, men designed and built 'flying' machines — but their attempts were thwarted at almost every turn.

The success of the gliders had already given these inventors the first clues to the ideal shape for their machines, but again the stumbling block was the power unit. The coming of the steam engine brought with it a glimmer of hope that the answer had been found, but this form of propulsion proved much too heavy for the frail craft, and at best

Bird Machine

De Groof Machine

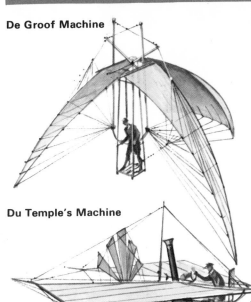

Du Temple's Machine

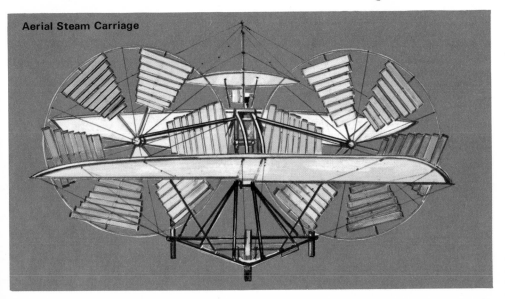

Even as late as 1865, there were still those who believed in 'bird-power.' An unknown American inventor submitted this design for a 'natural flying machine' to be lifted into the air by a group of captive brown eagles. He had heard that eagles could carry off sheep and reasoned that ten of them could lift a man.

The first powered aircraft to hop with a pilot on board was built by Felix du Temple, a French naval officer. Powered by a steam engine which rotated a fan propeller, it leaped then dropped to the ground, piloted by a young sailor in 1874.

Aerial Steam Carriage

In 1846, William Samuel Henson designed and built his Aerial Steam Carriage. He was inspired by Sir George Cayley's experiments in glider design, but his invention never got off the ground. The steam engine he installed was much too heavy.

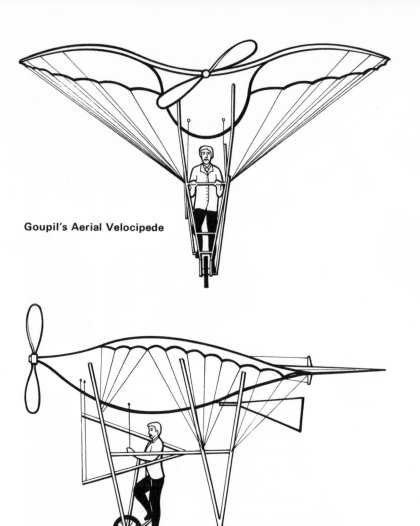

Goupil's Aerial Velocipede

could drive an airplane for only a short hop.

Some inventors tried to introduce battery-driven engines, but they too were cumbersome and messy and did not produce sufficient power to turn a propeller at a fast enough speed for take-off. It was a frustrating time for the inventors, who could sense that they were close to success.

Some of the 'aircraft' which emerged from these back-room workshops provoked nothing but laughter from onlookers, while others were respectfully treated to a few paragraphs in scientific magazines. The testing of a new machine on its maiden flight often brought sightseers out to enjoy the fun – and fun it was, for these fledgling flights invariably ended in a tangle of wreckage.

But the pioneering inventors refused to allow set-backs to dull their enthusiasm, and it was during this Victorian period that some of the weirdest designs of all came off the drawing board.

Goupil's Aerial Velocipede (cycle), built in 1885, demanded of the would-be pilot extraordinarily strong arms and legs. Unfortunately the pilot was utterly exhausted through pedalling before the craft could lift from the ground.

In 1883, a model of Professor Baranowski's Steam Flying Machine actually flew. It had flapping wings driven by a steam engine in the cigar-shaped hull. A propeller under each wing and one at the tail provided the forward power, while the craft was steered by two *ship's oars* at the rear. No full-size version was built.

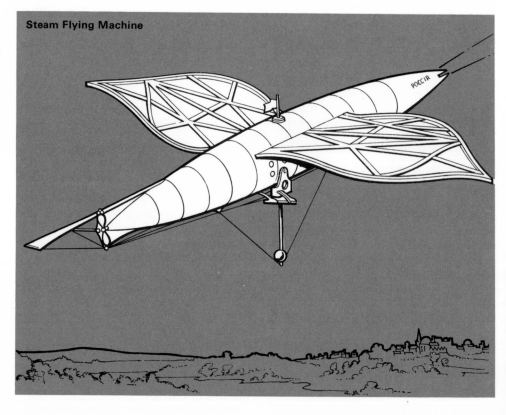

Steam Flying Machine

One inventor, an American whose name is not recorded in the history books, maintained an unswerving belief in the power of birds to get him airborne. He believed that by tethering them to his craft he could use their wing power to get him aloft.

But the accent was firmly upon steam-driven 'aerial carriages,' as they were known, and a succession of these were built, many of which made modest leaps into the air, like those of Felix du Temple, Thomas Moy and Ader Eole.

Their 'flights' were no more than hops and lacked any sort of control which would signify a breakthrough.

A Belgian inventor, called Vincent de Groof, shunned the steam engine in favor of the 'flapping wing' method. But experiments with his machine cost him his life when he leaped, flapping, from a hot-air balloon at a height of 1,000 feet.

There were those inventions which, short of a miracle, could never have got off the ground, like Doctor Ayres'

Designed and built by an American doctor, W. O. Ayres, in 1885, this contraption embodied a series of compressed air-driven propellers, supplemented by pedalled propellers and a hand-operated rudder. It did not fly.

Aerial Vessel

Cole's Aerial Vessel had a passenger compartment sandwiched between two balloons, which gave it lift. Four fan-like propellers driven by a steam engine were intended to give it directional movement, but it never flew.

machine, which sported no wings at all and relied upon a cluster of propellers for its lift.

This period of aerial experimentation was also the hey-day of the bicycle, and it is perhaps not surprising that at least one inventor should try to invent a cycle which could fly. It need hardly be said that it never got off the ground.

Experiments proved expensive both in life and limb and in money. In 1894, Sir Hiram Maxim spent $46,000, a fortune in those days, on a series of experiments with biplane and multi-wing aircraft which ran along twin lengths of rail. One of them made a brief hop — an insignificant achievement for such an enormous investment.

Aerial Cycle

The Aerial Cycle must rank among the most incredible of all the Victorian inventions. In 1888, its inventor shunned the advances being made with engines and produced this cycle, but it was a complete flop.

Disappointment was the constant companion of the inventors, but they were spurred on by the belief that success was but a hair's breadth away.

The turn of the century was at hand and with it came the moment that these pioneers had dreamed of for so long . . .

An Improved Airship

American John P. Holmes of Oak Valley, Kansas, dreamt up the idea of an Improved Airship in 1889. It is hardly surprising that his creation never left the ground for it would have demanded super-human leg and arm power of the pilot.

In 1894 Sir Hiram S. Maxim, a naturalized American, spent $46,000 on building this giant. It had a wing area of 4,000 square feet, ran on rails, had two 18-foot propellers and weighed 3½ tons. In spite of its size and weight, it actually lifted itself off the rails — only to come to an abrupt halt when it crashed. Further tests were abandoned.

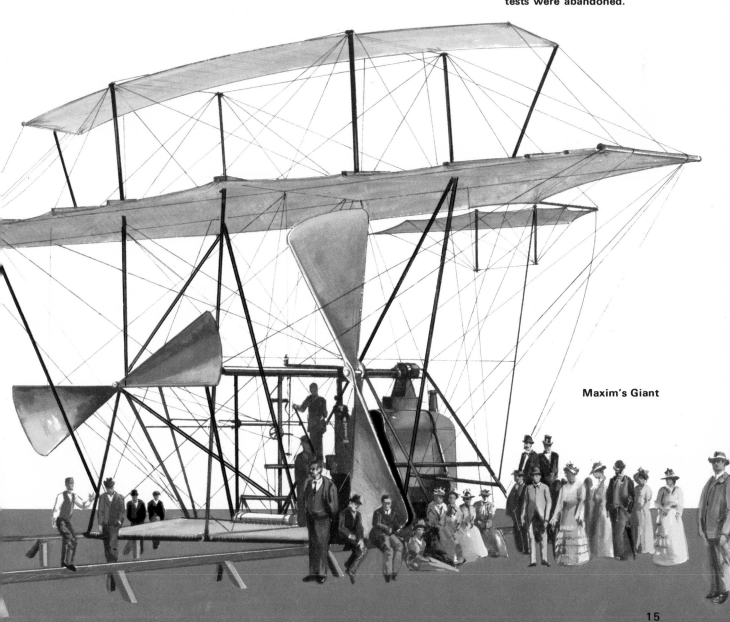

Maxim's Giant

First Powered Flights

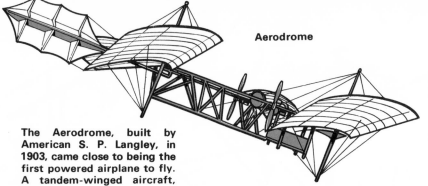

Aerodrome

The Aerodrome, built by American S. P. Langley, in 1903, came close to being the first powered airplane to fly. A tandem-winged aircraft, driven by a 52-hp gasoline engine, it twice crashed on take-off from a specially-built launching platform on the Potomac river.

Wind Tunnel

The Wright brothers built this small wind tunnel in which they tested a whole series of wing sections in order to arrive at the ideal shape for the wings of their gliders.

The greatest moment in aviation history arrived on December 17, 1903, when the Wright brothers' Flyer lifted into the air to become the first ever heavier-than-air, powered airplane to make a sustained and controlled flight. The epic flight took place at Kill Devil Hills, USA, with Orville at the controls.

The year 1903 brought with it the most significant advances in heavier-than-air powered and manned flight. The single factor which until then had dogged inventors of the airplane was the heavy engine, but then came the answer — the internal combustion gasoline engine.

The new engine was both light and packed more power in relation to its size.

In 1903, an American, S. P. Langley, installed a gasoline engine in his tandem-wing airplane design and came very close to achieving a 'first' in powered and manned flight. He devised a novel launching pad for his machine by converting a river houseboat into a take-off platform, but two attempted launches resulted only in a thorough soaking. Disheartened and short of funds, Langley gave up.

But there were other Americans hard at work, and in that very same year they achieved what, until then, had seemed impossible . . .

Orville and Wilbur Wright had, for many years, been engrossed in designing a glider, and they did so with considerable success, inspired in their quest by the experiments of Otto Lilienthal.

The Wrights discovered that there was one fundamental fault in Lilienthal's method of flying control, so they experimented with the 'warping wing' system, by which the wings could be 'twisted' to control the attitude of the glider flight. To their basic biplane glider, the *Flyer*, they added an internal combustion engine of their own design, which drove two propellers.

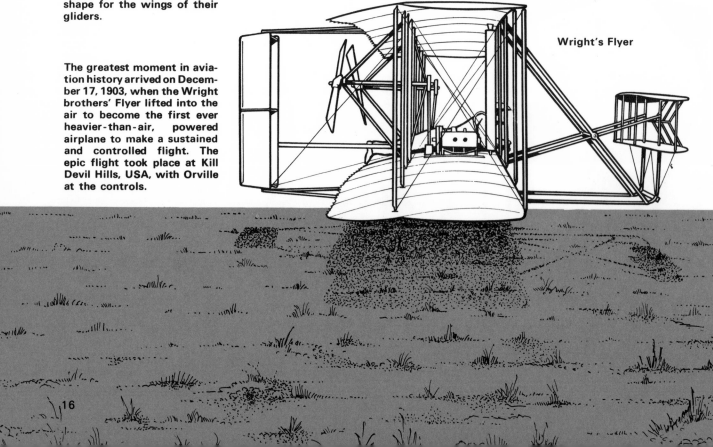

Wright's Flyer

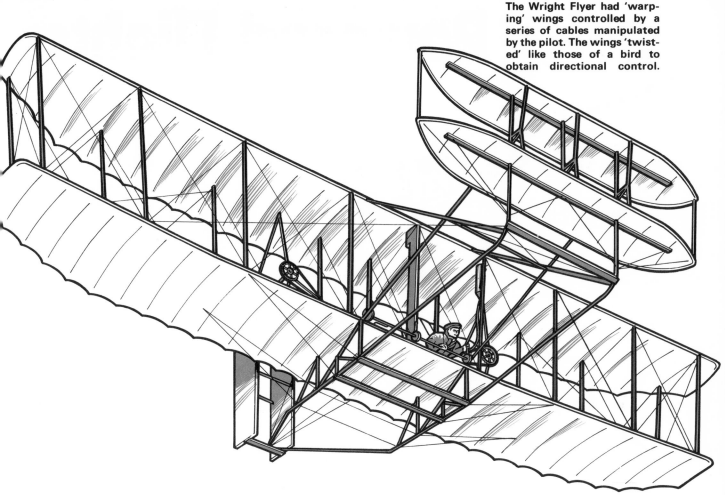

The Wright Flyer had 'warping' wings controlled by a series of cables manipulated by the pilot. The wings 'twisted' like those of a bird to obtain directional control.

minutes in an aircraft which could bank and turn with ease.

After that first flight of the *Flyer*, other designers followed with their versions. Santos Dumont, who had already built an airship, built and flew his *14 bis*, making the first powered, heavier-than-air flight in Europe.

From then on, successful designs poured off the drawing board. Then proof that the airplane was here to stay came in 1909 when a French airplane designer, Louis Bleriot, flew his single-engined monoplane across the English Channel.

The Wrights showed their versatility when they designed and helped to build their own 4-cylinder 12-hp engine for the Flyer.

The *Santos Dumont 14 bis* made the first powered flight in Europe. Built by the Brazilian Santos Dumont, it consisted of a series of box-kites and flew 'tail' first. Although its flight was short, it began a spate of successful flights in Europe.

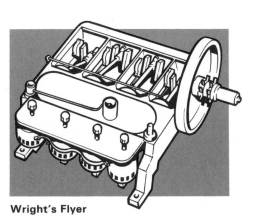

Wright's Flyer

The initial flight at Kitty Hawk, North Carolina, on December 14, 1903, ended in a crash. But they persevered, and three days later Orville made the very first powered and sustained flight in a heavier-than-air craft which lasted only 12 seconds and covered a mere 120 feet. But they had finally done it — and to prove that it was no fluke they made more flights, eventually achieving, in 1907, a flying time of no less than 45

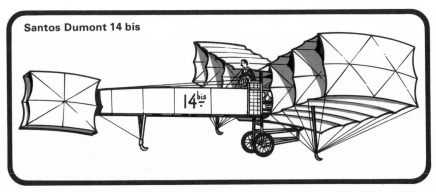

Santos Dumont 14 bis

Seaplanes & Flying Boats

Fabre Flying Boat

Frenchman Henri Fabre pioneered the idea of the float-plane which could take off from and land on water. His aircraft, which was equipped with floats, first flew in 1910. To fly the float-plane, Fabre sat perched on the open rectangular framework. It flew only once.

Henri Fabre flew the first seaplane at Martigues on March 28, 1910. His aircraft was a one-off 'freak,' but it stimulated other inventors to concentrate on seaplanes. The most successful of these men was an American, Glenn Curtiss.

Curtiss's early designs were not true seaplanes, but biplanes which took off from stagings fitted above the fore-decks of warships, the predecessor of the carrier-borne aircraft. His airplanes were fitted with emergency floatation tubes to prevent them sinking if they landed on the water.

Curtiss, hailed as the 'father' of the seaplane and flying-boat, eventually produced some remarkable designs, and it was he, more than any other, who pioneered this form of transport. In 1919, one of his seaplanes became the first to fly across the Atlantic, making stops on the way.

Since then some very unusual maritime airplanes have been built. One of these, the Italian *Savoia Marchetti S-55*, instead of having a single fuselage, consisted of two hull-shaped units in which passengers were housed.

Built in 1919 by the famous Italian Caprioni company, the *Ca 60 Transaero* was a giant with nine sets of wings, each with a span of 98 feet 6 inches. It had eight engines of 400 hp each, and was designed for trans-Atlantic flights.

The greatest of the early seaplane aviators was the American Glenn Curtiss, whose original aircraft were of conventional design but equipped with floats.

Ca 60 Transaero

Curtiss Hydro-aeroplane

**Short-Mayo Composite –
Maia and Mercury**

The Short-Mayo Composite's piggy-back system was devised to extend the range of an aircraft. So much fuel was used up in take-off that this method was adopted to give the smaller plane a helping hand into the air. The Maia, the larger of the two aircraft, took off with the Mercury on her back. Once airborne, they parted company and Mercury flew on to her destination.

Savoia Marchetti S-55

The Italian *Savoia Marchetti S-55* was a revolutionary twin-hull flying-boat, first flown in 1925. Eight years later, a squadron of these flying-boats made a spectacular trans-Atlantic formation flight. The crew occupied cockpits in the wing between the hulls.

Built by the American Grumman company, the JF-2 float-plane was an amphibian, capable of taking off from and landing on water.

In the 1920s and 1930s, great strides were made in opening mail and passenger services across the oceans, and it was the flying-boats that pioneered these long-distance routes.

Giant flying-boats were built, but some, like the *Caprioni Ca 60*, were so heavy that, far from being able to fly the Atlantic, they could not even get off the water.

Other monsters, such as the multi-engined *Dornier Do X*, met with better fortune, but even this had to be scrapped because it could not fly high enough.

Achieving the desired long range

JF-2

With its 157-foot wing span, the 12-engined Dornier Do X flying boat was one of the 'jumbos' of the 1930s. The Swiss-built prototype made an epic flight from Germany to New York and back in 1930. Capable of carrying 169 passengers, it had a range of 1,740 miles. It was eventually scrapped because of its limited height capability.

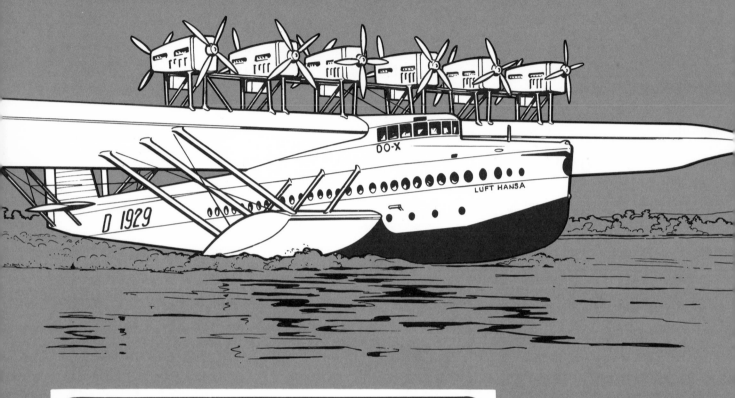

RFB (Lippisch) X113-AM

The experimental single-seat *RFB (Lippisch) X113-AM* is perhaps one of the most unusual of the modern designs. Trials with this fiber glass aerofoil aircraft began in 1970 on Lake Constance and proved successful.

of the flying-boat posed the cardinal problem for the designers, but in one case this was overcome in a rather novel way, using the *Short-Mayo Composite* (piggy-back) where the larger aircraft gave the small seaplane a 'lift' into the air to conserve fuel on take-off.

Throughout the Second World War, flying-boats were employed on maritime reconnaissance and anti-submarine duties. After the war, with the advent of the long-range land-based aircraft, the flying-boat lost its commercial appeal. But there were still those who believed in them . . .

Island Aircraft Spectra

The American Island Aircraft Spectra is a light amphibian research aeroplane which can carry four passengers. The wings are canted downwards to serve as stabilising 'floats' when on the water.

In Britain, the Sanders Roe company built the giant 10-engined *Princess* flying-boat, the 'airplane nobody wanted.' And in America, in 1947, millionaire Howard Hughes dreamed up the *Hercules*, an all-wooden flying-boat with a wing span of 320 feet, the biggest airplane ever to fly. It made one 1,000 yard hop off Long Beach harbor and never flew again.

The age of the flying-boat had, it seemed, come to an end. Certainly no more 'giants' were built, but in recent years there has been a resurgence of interest in both seaplanes and flying-boats, although these are almost all small sporting or experimental aircraft.

Float-planes continue to operate between the isolated outposts in the dense forests of Canada, where the only 'landing grounds' are huge lakes.

The Pereira GP2 Osprey 1 flying-boat is the brain-child of an American designer. A lightweight single-seat aircraft, it can be built at home, complete with trailer for towing it to the water. Made of wood, it is powered by a 90-hp engine and first flew in 1970.

Pereira GP2 Osprey 1

Fighters

Sage Type 2

The Sage Type 2, first flown in 1916, was one of the few fighters to have an enclosed cockpit. It was equipped with a Lewis gun operated by the observer, who sat to the rear of the pilot. To fire his gun, the observer had to stand upright with his head and shoulders protruding through the hole in the upper wing.

Fighters, probably more than any other type of aircraft, have undergone the greatest changes in design. Beginning as hastily improvised adaptations of reconnaissance aircraft in the First World War, they have evolved over almost 70 years to the supersonic swing-wing and jump-jet wonders of today. During that development, a strange array of fighters has taken to the air.

The first air conflicts were fought over the battle trenches of Northern Europe, shortly after the outbreak of the First World War. There were no fighter planes as such, only flimsy wood-and-canvas reconnaissance aircraft which flew on 'spotting' missions over the enemy lines.

The aircraft did not become a fighting machine until some adventurous pilots armed themselves with a weird assortment of weapons, including shot-guns, pistols and even *darts*! Finding these largely ineffective, they went a stage further and fixed machine-guns to their

A.D. Scout

spotter planes, intent upon shooting down enemy aircraft. This was the turning point which meant the beginning of the bitter dog-fights.

The addition of the machine-gun in those early days was not without its hazards. The observer, who generally acted as a gunner as well as spotter, often had to stand erect in his cockpit to fire the weapon.

On one occasion a British airman, Captain Strange, actually fell out of his

The A.D. Scout prototype biplane fighter first flew in 1915. To get all-around forward vision, the pilot sat in front of the 100-hp Gnome 'pusher' engine. The wings were set behind the pilot to give him a clear downward view. Like most aircraft of its time, it was built of wood and only partially covered with fabric.

The Blackburn Triplane was one of the first fighters with three sets of wings. Although it is said to have made a speed of 115 mph, it was scrapped as a warplane and only the prototype was built.

Blackburn Triplane

Arsenal-Delanne 10

The French *Arsenal-Delanne 10,* first flown just before the Second World War, was a biplane with a difference. It had no tail as such, but the lower wing was set at the rear of the aircraft below the two-seat cockpit.

Not to be out-done by the triplanes, the Wight Quadruplane sported four sets of wings, the lowest set slightly shorter than the others. Only one of these aircraft was ever built.

machine when it overturned while he was changing the ammunition drum on his Lewis gun. He escaped death only by hanging on to the gun until the aircraft righted itself.

Both Allied and German designers set their minds to building airplanes specifically for the role of fighting, and the planes that emerged on both sides were truly remarkable in shape and construction . . .

There were the 'pushers,' with their engines and propellers situated behind the pilot and observer in order to give both of them a clear view ahead and a wide forward angle of fire.

Aircraft designers in France, Britain and Germany tried every conceivable variation of design to improve the fighting performance of their aircraft. There were monoplanes, biplanes, triplanes — and even quadruplanes! Some were highly successful while others proved miserable failures.

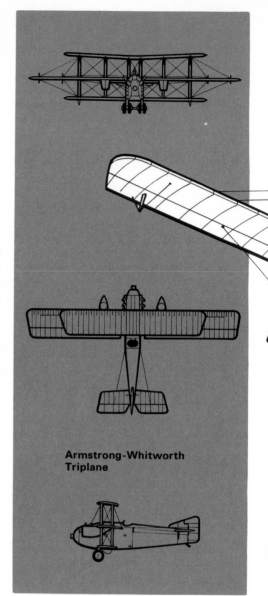

Armstrong-Whitworth Triplane

Flying fighters in those early days demanded great skill and courage from pilot and observer. Machines were fickle and a steep dive or sudden manoeuvre could result in the airplane shedding its wings, with fatal consequences.

Machine-guns had no interrupter gears to prevent them shooting off parts of the aircraft or the propellers. It was, in fact, commonplace for pilots to return from missions with fuselages torn to shreds by their own bullets!

Slender, exposed control lines operating elevators and ailerons were prone to snapping, while the primitive engines were dogged by mechanical failure.

Until the advent of the forward-firing machine-gun, which shot its bullets between the propeller blades by means of linking its mechanism to that of the engine, guns had to be housed well away from the blades, hence the

Wight Quadruplane

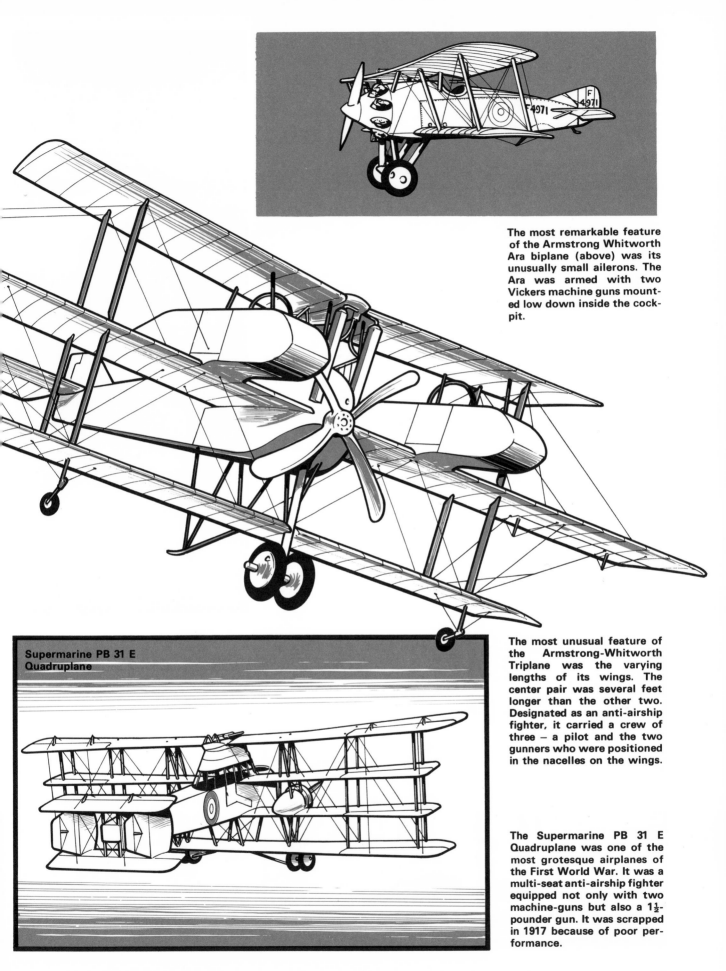

The most remarkable feature of the Armstrong Whitworth Ara biplane (above) was its unusually small ailerons. The Ara was armed with two Vickers machine guns mounted low down inside the cockpit.

The most unusual feature of the Armstrong-Whitworth Triplane was the varying lengths of its wings. The center pair was several feet longer than the other two. Designated as an anti-airship fighter, it carried a crew of three — a pilot and the two gunners who were positioned in the nacelles on the wings.

The Supermarine PB 31 E Quadruplane was one of the most grotesque airplanes of the First World War. It was a multi-seat anti-airship fighter equipped not only with two machine-guns but also a 1½-pounder gun. It was scrapped in 1917 because of poor performance.

Supermarine PB 31 E Quadruplane

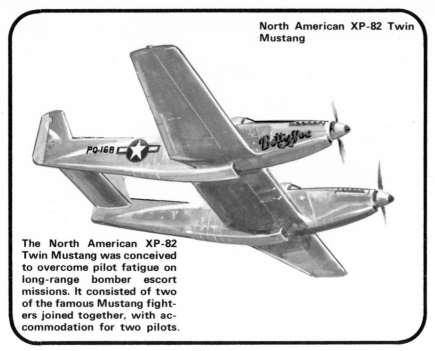

The North American XP-82 Twin Mustang was conceived to overcome pilot fatigue on long-range bomber escort missions. It consisted of two of the famous Mustang fighters joined together, with accommodation for two pilots.

popularity of the pusher type engine.

With few exceptions, cockpits were open to the elements, allowing wind, rain and cold to get to the crew, and making flying extremely uncomfortable.

So frail and light were these fledgling fighters that parachutes were not provided lest their weight and bulk should impair the performance of the airplane.

Fighter design progressed throughout the inter-war years, but with the coming of the Second World War design and construction took on a new impetus. Already the jet and rocket engines had been born. Designs, many of which look comic alongside today's supersonic jets, appeared in prototype and then went into operational service. Rocket interceptors, like the German *Me 163 Komet* with its operational endurance of only *eight* minutes, wrought havoc among American daylight bombers.

Scores of British *Meteor* jet fighters were produced and played an important role in combating the German rocket attacks on British cities.

The novel *Dornier 335V*, with its propellers at both front and rear, was born only to die an early death.

Flown for the first time in 1943, the German *Dornier Do 335V* was a single-seat fighter-bomber. Its most unusual characteristics were its 'pusher' and 'puller' propellers at tail and nose, and the downward-pointing tail fins. Although ten were delivered to the German Luftwaffe (Air Force), none was used operationally.

The German *Messerschmitt Me 163 Komet* single-seat interceptor aircraft was the most revolutionary fighter used in action in the Second World War. Powered by a rocket engine, it scored many successes against enemy bombers. It first flew in 1941, but was not operational until much later. With a speed of 596 mph, it could operate for only *eight* minutes.

Dornier Do 335V

Messerschmitt Me 163 Komet

Curtiss Ascender

278846

Another single-seat interceptor was the Curtiss Ascender, which incorporated some quite unusual features. First flown in 1941, it had swept wings with fins at the tips and a pusher engine which could produce a top speed of 390 mph. It did not go into squadron service.

The famous Curtiss company of America built the *Ascender* with swept-back wings, a feature which was to become common in both fighter and bomber aircraft of later years.

The fighter has changed out of all recognition from the spluttering strutters of the First World War.

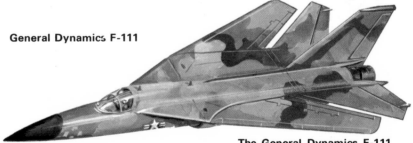

General Dynamics F-111

The General Dynamics F-111 is a multi-role aircraft which can be used as a fighter, fighter-bomber or reconnaissance aircraft. It was the first supersonic swing-wing airplane to go into operational service. The wings are fully extended outwards for take-off and landing, but swept back for high speeds. It first flew in 1967.

An adaptation of the famous Meteor jet fighter was the experimental WK935, used for test purposes. The pilot in the forward cockpit lay in a prone position to fly the aircraft.

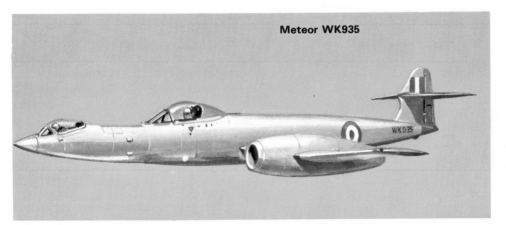

Meteor WK935

WK935

Bombers

In 1913, Igor Sikorsky built the world's first 4-engined bomber, the *Ilya Mourometz*. Of the 70 bombers of this type made, only one was lost in 400 raids carried out in the First World War. The *Mourometz* had a top speed of only 70 mph, a range of 300 miles, and could carry 1,500 lb of bombs. It required a crew of seven.

Ilya Mourometz

Since their introduction, bomber aircraft, like fighters, have undergone considerable changes, not only in design but also in bomb-load capacity.

When the real potential of the bomber was realized soon after the outbreak of the First World War, efforts were quickly made to use existing spotter aircraft in this role. On reconnaissance missions, crews took with them several hand grenades which they dropped into enemy trenches – usually with very little accuracy. In order to hit their targets they had to fly very low, and

this more often than not brought a hail of fire from the ground, occasionally resulting in damage to the aircraft.

Igor Sikorsky, the Russian aircraft designer, had already built the world's first 4-engined aircraft, the *Le Grand*, and he converted this into a highly-successful bomber, renamed the *Ilya Mourometz*.

Bomber aircraft were built on both sides, but it must be said that they were largely ineffective because of the small pay-load they could carry and the inaccuracy of their bombing.

The French Breguet B.M.5 could accommodate a bomb-load of only 650 lb, not enough to do any really serious damage, particularly since bomb-

The French *Breguet B.M.5* two-seat reconnaissance bomber was the first to carry a 35-mm cannon. Used mainly at night, it carried out raids from late 1916 onwards. It could carry 650 lb of bombs.

Breguet B.M.5

The German *Heinkel He 111Z*, nicknamed the 'siamese twin,' was used during the Second World War for towing heavy gliders. It consisted of two twin-engined Heinkel bombers linked together, with an additional fifth engine mounted in the center wing between the fuselages. The pilot and co-pilot were accommodated in individual cockpits.

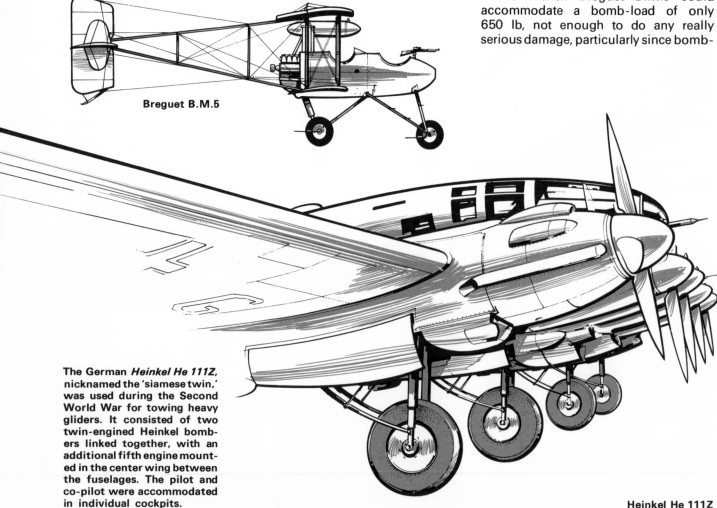

Heinkel He 111Z

Amiot 143M

In 1946, just after the end of the Second World War, the American Northrop YB-35 Flying Wing bomber made its appearance. Fifteen of these were built, but subsequently taken out of service. Twelve were powered by 3,500-hp Pratt & Whitney R-4360 engines and the others by turbojets.

The German Blohm und Voss company was noted for its unconventional aircraft, but none they produced during the Second World War matched their BV 141 as an oddity. This short-range reconnaissance aircraft had its cockpit mounted 'on the wing,' and in one version of this type had only half a tailplane. None of the versions of this aircraft went into operational service.

Northrop YB-35 Flying Wing

World War, further advances were made when the conflict ended. With this further development came oddities like the *Northrop Flying Wing* and the 6-engined *Convair B-36*, which required a crew of *fifteen* to man it.

With the introduction of the intercontinental ballistic missile, the bomber is all but a thing of the past. But in the last war it was the bomber which helped tip the scales in favor of the Allies.

aiming was largely a matter of 'pot luck.'

German *Gotha* bombers carried out 'terror' raids on English cities when they superseded the mighty Zeppelin airships in their attacks on London.

By 1918, the British Handley Page company produced the *0/400*, which could carry a single 1,650 lb bomb, the largest used in the war.

It was not until the Second World War that the opposing sides brought into the fray really effective bombers coupled with accurate bomb-aiming devices. Airplanes like the British *Wellington*, *Halifax* and *Lancaster*, the American *Liberator*, *B-17* and *B-29 Superfortress*, bristling with guns and carrying a huge pay-load.

Based on knowledge gained in bomber production during the Second

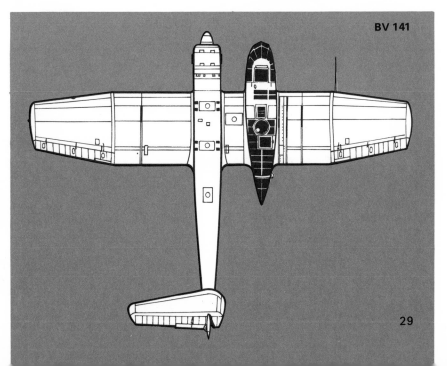

BV 141

Passenger & Freight Aircraft

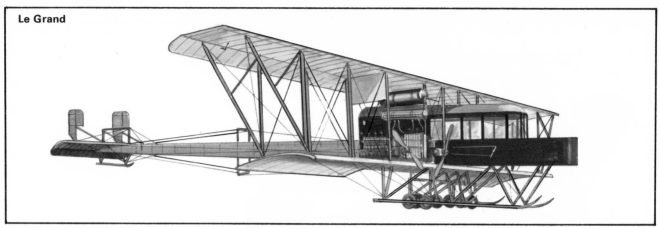
Le Grand

Igor Sikorsky's *Le Grand* achieved more than one 'first.' Built in 1912/13, this biplane was the largest heavier-than-air plane of its time, with a wingspan of 92 feet. It was both the first 4-engined aircraft and the first to have an enclosed passenger cabin. It had an open nose, accessible through a front door in the cabin. In the passenger cabin were four seats, a sofa, a table and a washroom.

One of the first all-metal passenger aircraft, the Handley Page HP 42 first flew in 1930. It could carry 24 passengers on long distance trips and 38 on short-haul services. Eight of these saw service for nine years with Imperial Airways and flew some ten million miles.

The first passenger-carrying aircraft were balloons and airships, but both these forms of transport had their drawbacks. They were slow, difficult to control, and their performance was greatly impaired by adverse weather conditions. The answer to these difficulties, at least in part, came with the introduction of the heavier-than-air airplane.

It seems hardly credible that, only *nine* years after the first powered aircraft had flown, a *four-engined* passenger airplane made its debut. It was the Russian *Le Grand*, the design of the world's foremost aviator, Igor Sikorsky. He was not only a brilliant designer but also a man of great vision. He foresaw the day when airplanes carrying passengers would 'shrink' the globe with international passenger routes.

The giant *Le Grand* was equipped with every modern convenience for the passengers, including comfortable seats, a sofa, wardrobe and washroom — all enclosed in the first ever passenger cabin. When war came, the *Le Grand* was converted into a bomber and carried out many bombing raids.

Throughout the war, bigger and better bombers were built. Then, with the war over, the same bombers were converted for civilian passenger use. Aircraft like the *Vickers Vimy*, in which Alcock and Brown flew the Atlantic non-stop, were transformed into passenger and freight-carrying aircraft. Another such bomber, the French *Farman Goliath*, was re-designed internally.

Designers continued with the high standard of pre-war interior design. Flying was expensive and the wealthy passengers demanded luxury accom-

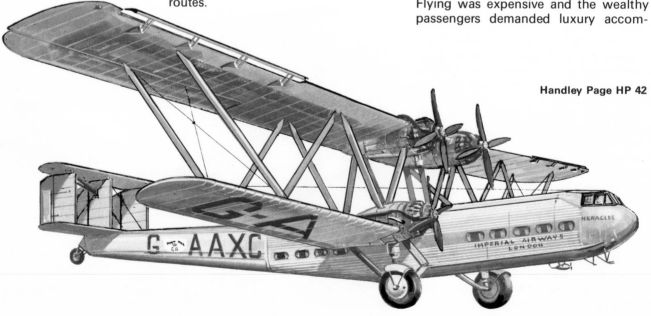
Handley Page HP 42

DeHavilland DH 34

G-EBBS

The British DeHavilland DH 34 was another of the pioneer airliners. The passenger compartment was luxuriously decorated and could seat 11 people. Powered by a 450-hp Napier Lion engine, it could cruise at 105 mph with a range of 365 miles.

modation — which they got. Unlike the modern airliner, which has row upon row of cramped seats, these early passenger planes carried fewer passengers and were spacious and luxurious, resembling the first-class saloon of an ocean liner.

But while the passengers lounged in splendid, if bumpy, surroundings, the crew did not. Most early airliners had open cockpits where the pilot and co-pilot had to brave the elements.

Because of the still limited range of the land-based plane, flying-boats enjoyed a hey-day of passenger service — but then came the Second World War . . .

During that war, multi-engined bombers were produced and advances made in warplane design. When the war ended, these technical advances were applied to civilian aircraft.

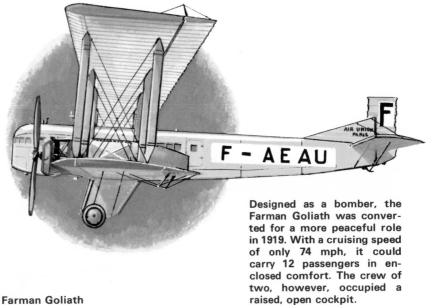

Farman Goliath

F - AE AU

Designed as a bomber, the Farman Goliath was converted for a more peaceful role in 1919. With a cruising speed of only 74 mph, it could carry 12 passengers in enclosed comfort. The crew of two, however, occupied a raised, open cockpit.

31

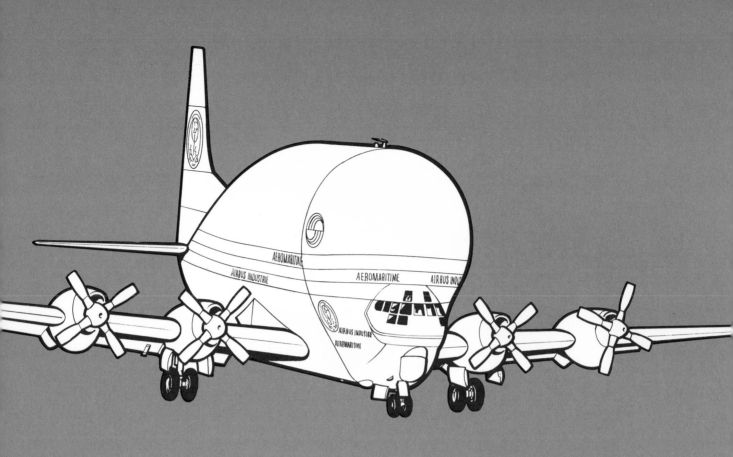

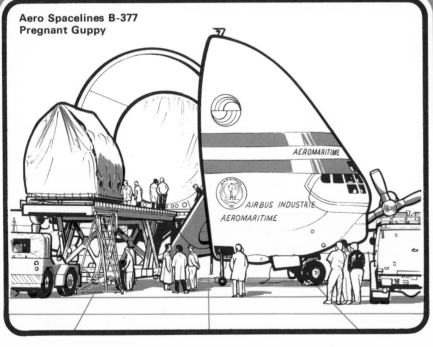

The Aero Spacelines B-377 Pregnant Guppy has been described as the most grotesque aircraft ever designed. It was originally converted from the basic Boeing Strato- cruiser design and was built to carry booster stages of America's moon rockets from the works to the launch area.

Bigger and faster aircraft were built which could carry in excess of 100 passengers. Sub-sonic jets, like the *Comet*, *VC-10* and *Boeing 707*, slashed flying time on the international routes.

These same planes, stripped of their seats, could carry large cargoes to the far-reaching corners of the globe.

Then came the giants, the *Jumbo* jet and the *Galaxy*, two of the biggest airplanes in the world, along with specialist aircraft like the *Pregnant Guppy*, designed to transport sections of the huge American moon rockets . . . a very far cry from the wood-and-canvas pioneering passenger and freight air- planes of 60 years ago.

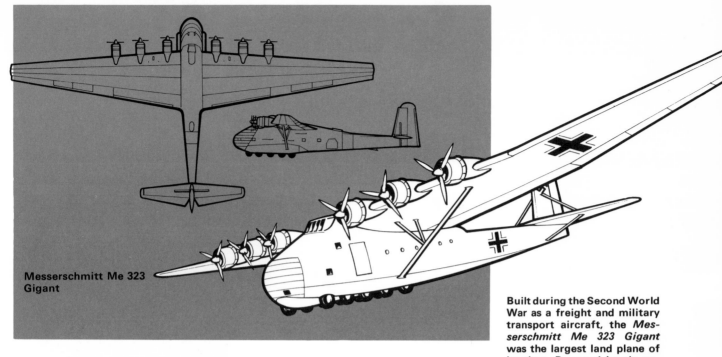

**Messerschmitt Me 323
Gigant**

Built during the Second World
War as a freight and military
transport aircraft, the *Messerschmitt Me 323 Gigant*
was the largest land plane of
its time. Powered by six engines, it is said to have been
capable of carrying a railway
carriage. Its nose opened up
to allow entry of freight. It
was originally developed
from a glider design, and had
ten landing wheels.

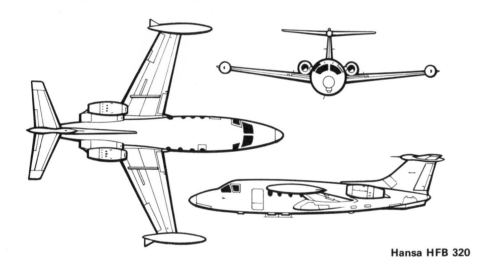

Hansa HFB 320

The *Hansa HFB 320* twin-jet,
with its unusual forward-
sweep wings, is basically an
executive aircraft, although it
has fulfilled a wide variety of
roles including freighter, tar-
get tow and aerial survey aircraft. First flown in 1964, the
passenger version can carry
12 people.

Sporting Aircraft

The Gee Bee Super Sportster was more engine than airplane. The concept was the minimum airframe accommodating the maximum size engine. In 1932, this 800-hp driven Sportster won the Thomson Trophy race at a speed of 252·7 mph

Gee Bee Super Sportster

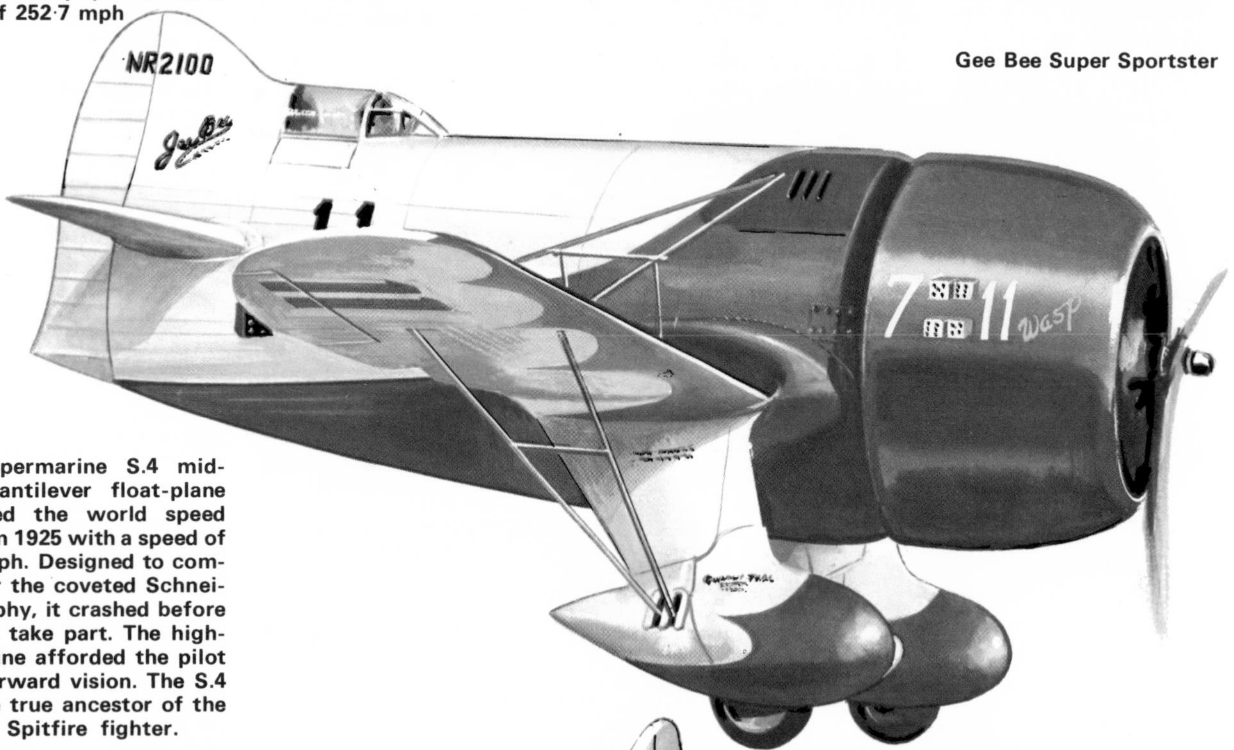

The Supermarine S.4 mid-wing cantilever float-plane shattered the world speed record in 1925 with a speed of 226·6 mph. Designed to compete for the coveted Schneider Trophy, it crashed before it could take part. The high-set engine afforded the pilot little forward vision. The S.4 was the true ancestor of the famous Spitfire fighter.

Supermarine S.4

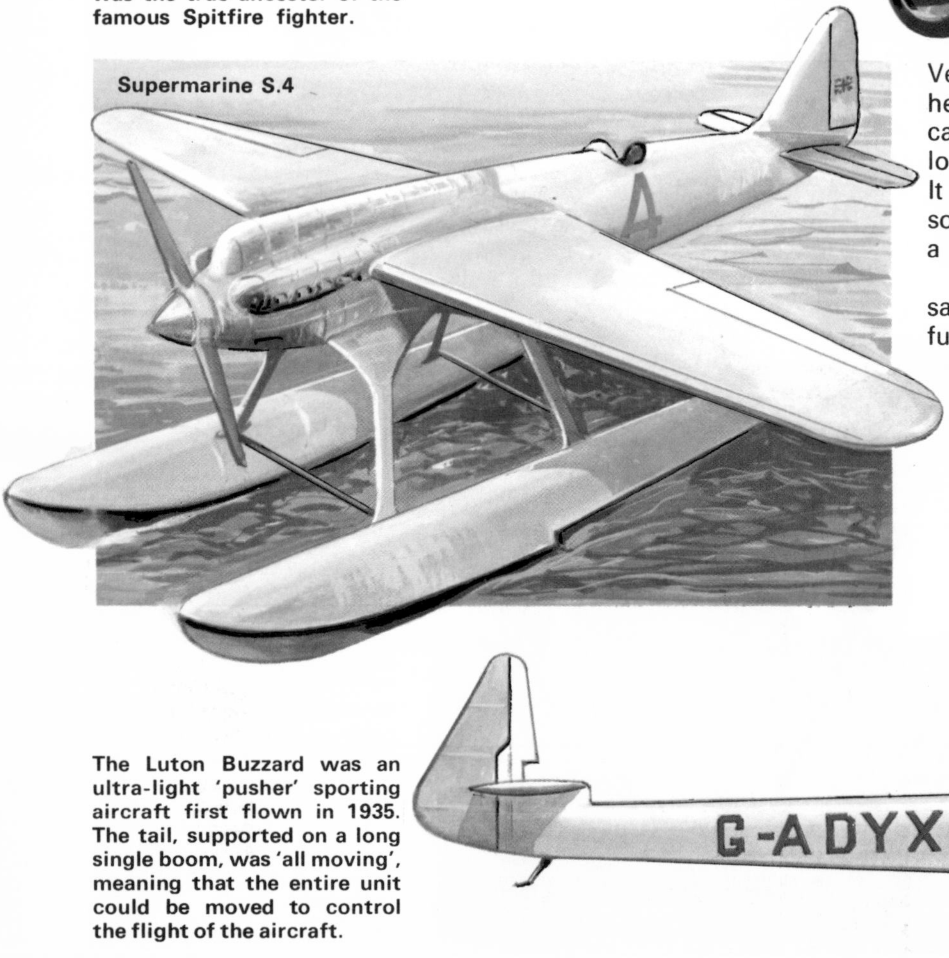

Very soon after its introduction, the heavier-than-air powered airplane became the play-thing of rich young men longing for fresh fields of excitement. It was a new and thrilling experience to soar through the air, dicing with death — a brand new form of sport.

Although airplanes are infinitely safer today, the tradition of flying for fun and as a competitive sport has

The Luton Buzzard was an ultra-light 'pusher' sporting aircraft first flown in 1935. The tail, supported on a long single boom, was 'all moving', meaning that the entire unit could be moved to control the flight of the aircraft.

G-ADYX

Mig-8 Utka (Duck)

The Russian *Mig-8 Utka* (Duck) was an experimental light aircraft built in 1945/46 to test the tail first configuration with a pusher propeller, but this was found to be no better than the conventional design. Only one prototype was built.

The American Lesher Nomad matched other unusual sporting airplanes with its unconventional inverted tail fin and pusher propeller.

continued over the years. More and more civilians are learning to fly in their spare time. Some join clubs and hire aircraft, but there are still those who are not content simply to fly an airplane — they want to build their own aircraft as well.

Like the model airplane builder who buys a kit from a shop, the sporting flier can do likewise and buy a complete kit from a manufacturer for assembly at

Lesher Nomad

N1066Z

Flying Flea

G-AEGD

The Flying Flea, designed and built in 1933 by Frenchman Henri Mignet, was one of the most popular mini-planes ever built. Mignet's own Flea flew successfully, but then others tried to imitate him using inferior engines and materials with dismal results. But sense prevailed and today Fleas are still flying. Fore and aft control of this great little airplane was achieved by tilting the wing.

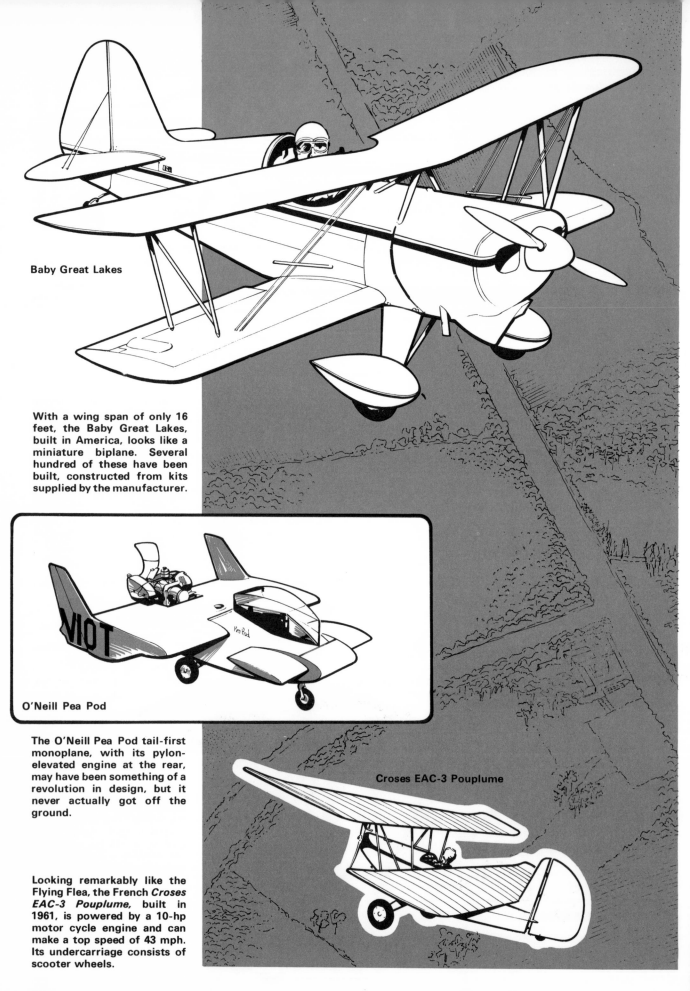

Baby Great Lakes

With a wing span of only 16 feet, the Baby Great Lakes, built in America, looks like a miniature biplane. Several hundred of these have been built, constructed from kits supplied by the manufacturer.

O'Neill Pea Pod

The O'Neill Pea Pod tail-first monoplane, with its pylon-elevated engine at the rear, may have been something of a revolution in design, but it never actually got off the ground.

Croses EAC-3 Pouplume

Looking remarkably like the Flying Flea, the French *Croses EAC-3 Pouplume,* built in 1961, is powered by a 10-hp motor cycle engine and can make a top speed of 43 mph. Its undercarriage consists of scooter wheels.

home. Others prefer to design and build their own sporting aircraft, fashioned to their own specifications and requirements.

These aircraft are a breed apart from all others. Many are quite unique. They are, almost without exception, 'minis,' some of which have engines as large as the rest of the aircraft. They are invariably the 'tiny-tots' of the aviation world, and on these pages you can see a few of them.

Baker Delta Kitten

The Baker Delta Kitten, built in 1962, resembles two triangles fitted horizontally together. The pilot sits 'in the tail.'

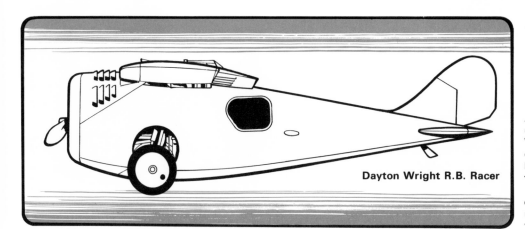

Dayton Wright R.B. Racer

Apart from its obviously unusual design, the Dayton Wright R.B. Racer had another peculiarity – the pilot had no forward vision and therefore could not see where he was going! The airplane did, however, fly and could make a speed of 200 mph. It was built in 1920.

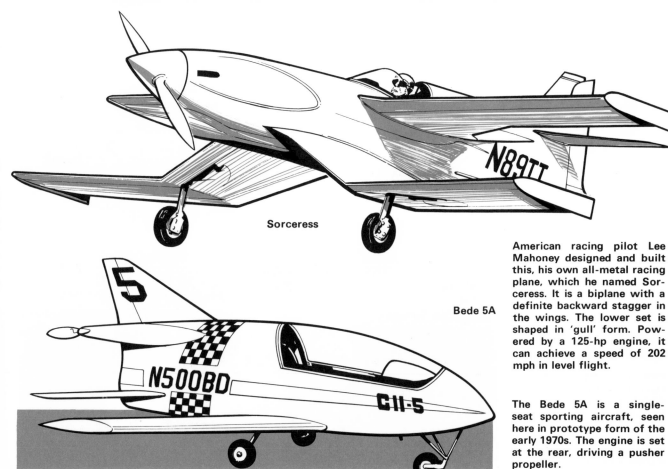

Sorceress

Bede 5A

American racing pilot Lee Mahoney designed and built this, his own all-metal racing plane, which he named Sorceress. It is a biplane with a definite backward stagger in the wings. The lower set is shaped in 'gull' form. Powered by a 125-hp engine, it can achieve a speed of 202 mph in level flight.

The Bede 5A is a single-seat sporting aircraft, seen here in prototype form of the early 1970s. The engine is set at the rear, driving a pusher propeller.

37

Helicopters & Autogyros

About the year 1490, Leonardo da Vinci drew up plans for this helicopter. It took the form of a rotating spiral vane which would screw itself vertically into the air. It was never built, but even if it had been it would not have flown.

Da Vinci's helicopter

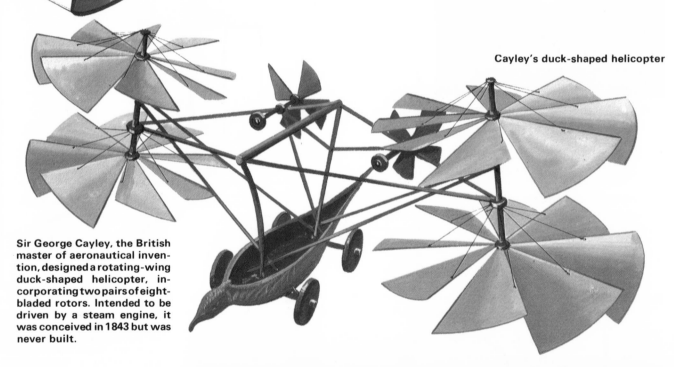

Leonardo da Vinci was the first man to seriously consider the possibility of a vertical take-off helicopter. He drew plans for a rotating spiral vane which could screw itself straight up into the air. His aircraft was never built, but even if it had been it would never have flown, for his basic theory of vertical take-off was faulty.

When fixed-wing airplanes began to come into their own at the beginning of this century, the problem of finding suitable runways presented itself. Long fields were needed for take-off, thus using up valuable agricultural land.

Vertical take-off seemed like the answer, and designers turned their thoughts to developing a helicopter.

The principle of vertical take-off and landing was first really appreciated by two Frenchmen who built the *Breguet-Richet Gyroplane 1* in 1907. It certainly lifted off the ground, but it had to be steadied by four men.

The initiative was taken up again by another Frenchman, Paul Cornu, who, in the same year, built and flew a tandem rotor machine. Unfortunately lack of money forced him to abandon his experiments.

Cayley's duck-shaped helicopter

Sir George Cayley, the British master of aeronautical invention, designed a rotating-wing duck-shaped helicopter, incorporating two pairs of eight-bladed rotors. Intended to be driven by a steam engine, it was conceived in 1843 but was never built.

Paul Cornu's tandem-rotor machine

In 1907, two of the most significant advances were made in helicopter design when the Frenchmen Cornu and Breguet-Richet built and flew the forerunners of today's helicopters. Both Paul Cornu's tandem-rotor machine and the *Breguet-Richet Gyroplane* lifted into the air during demonstrations.

Autogiro

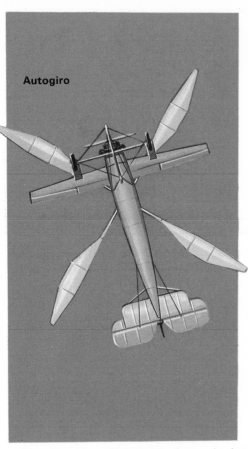

The 'father' of the helicopter, Igor Sikorsky, built this machine, one of his original designs, as early as 1910.

Sikorsky's helicopter

But it was a Spaniard, Juan de la Cierva, who came closest to vertical take-off when he built and flew his *Autogiro*. Resembling a conventional monoplane, it had a free-rotating four-blade rotor mounted on a 'pylon.' As the *Autogiro* ran along the runway, powered by the engine in the nose, the free-rotating blades spun round, giving it additional lift and a much shorter take-off run.

The original *Autogiro* was not without its problems. It tended to slew sideways, and it was not until Cierva

VS-300

A Spanish engineer, Juan de la Cierva, designed, built and flew his Autogiro in 1923. It looked not unlike a conventional airplane in basic design, but had free-rotating blades mounted on a pylon above the cockpit. These blades gave it its short take-off distance.

In 1940, Sikorsky built the VS-300 of steel tubing. It was powered by a 300-hp engine driving a three-blade main rotor with an anti-torque rotor on the tail. It was his first really successful helicopter. A fabric-covered nose was later added to protect the pilot from the elements and to streamline its looks.

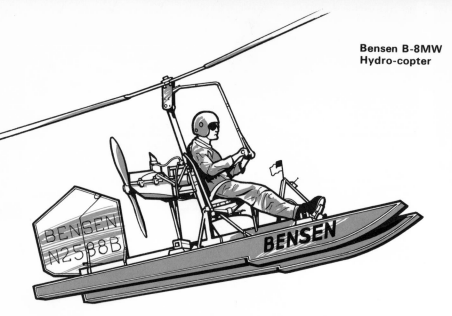

**Bensen B-8MW
Hydro-copter**

developed the 'flapping' rotor, in which the rotor blades were hinged at the roots, that he overcame the difficulty in later models.

The brilliant Igor Sikorsky had tested various helicopter designs as early as 1910, but it was not until 1940 that he produced his *VS-300*, built of steel tubing and powered by a 75-hp Lycoming engine. He incorporated an 'anti-torque' rotor on the tail, which prevented the craft from swinging around on its own axis, a problem helicopter designers had previously faced and failed to overcome. An improved version, the *R-4*, was the aircraft which became the foundation for the world's helicopter industry. Since then, helicopters and

The Bensen B-8MW Hydro-copter is a water-borne craft specially designed for the home builder. Powered by a 90-hp engine, it is basically an autogyro fitted with floats for operation off and on to water. It was first flown in 1955.

Bensen Sky-Mat

From the same stable, the Bensen Sky-Mat is equipped with ten independent rotors, each powered by a 10-hp engine. First flown in 1961, it was primarily intended for crop spraying.

The German *TRS-111 Gyroflug* is powered by a two-blade pusher propeller and a single rotor. Its most outstanding feature is its superb lines. This single-seat aircraft can take off in only 197 feet and make a maximum speed of 180 mph.

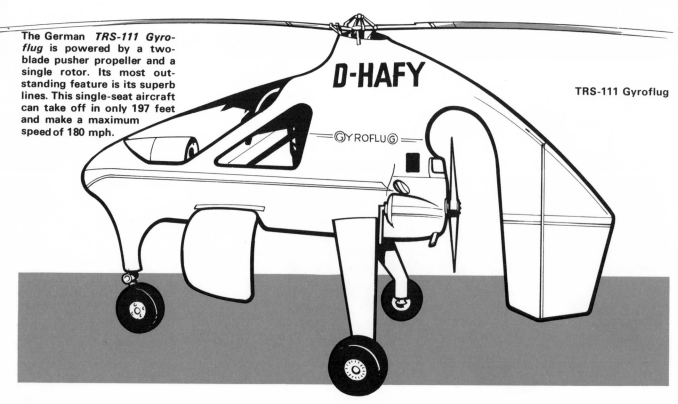

TRS-111 Gyroflug

D-HAFY

GYROFLUG

Sikorsky S-64

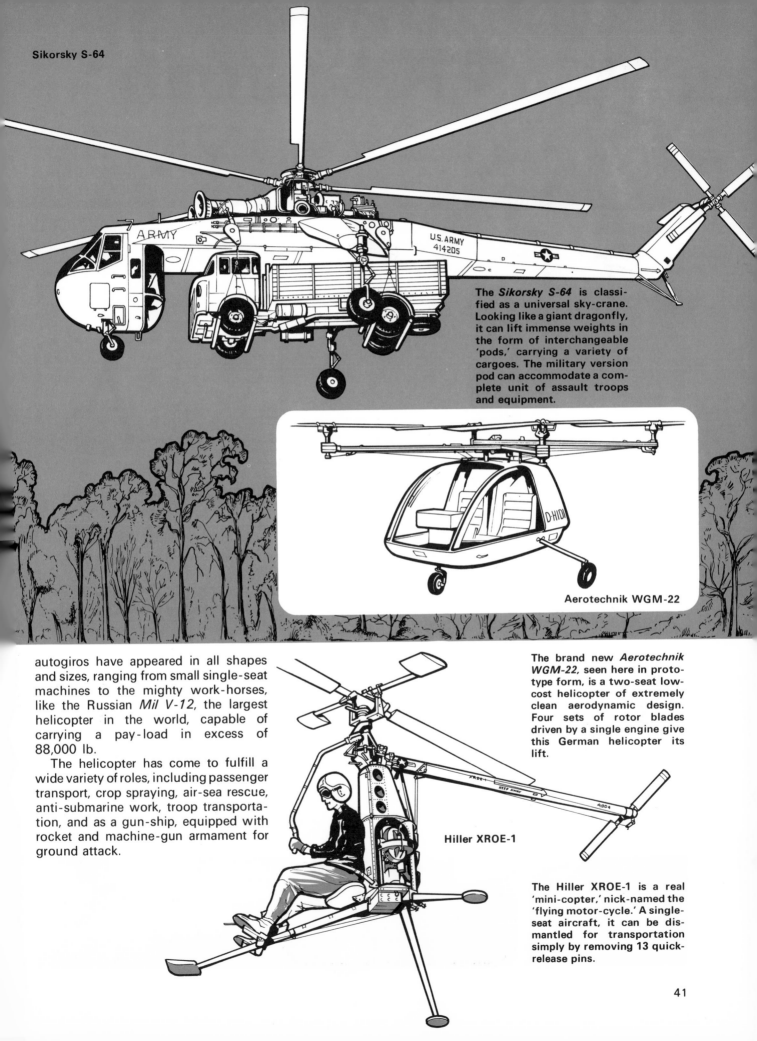

The *Sikorsky S-64* is classified as a universal sky-crane. Looking like a giant dragonfly, it can lift immense weights in the form of interchangeable 'pods,' carrying a variety of cargoes. The military version pod can accommodate a complete unit of assault troops and equipment.

Aerotechnik WGM-22

autogiros have appeared in all shapes and sizes, ranging from small single-seat machines to the mighty work-horses, like the Russian *Mil V-12*, the largest helicopter in the world, capable of carrying a pay-load in excess of 88,000 lb.

The helicopter has come to fulfill a wide variety of roles, including passenger transport, crop spraying, air-sea rescue, anti-submarine work, troop transportation, and as a gun-ship, equipped with rocket and machine-gun armament for ground attack.

The brand new *Aerotechnik WGM-22*, seen here in prototype form, is a two-seat low-cost helicopter of extremely clean aerodynamic design. Four sets of rotor blades driven by a single engine give this German helicopter its lift.

Hiller XROE-1

The Hiller XROE-1 is a real 'mini-copter,' nick-named the 'flying motor-cycle.' A single-seat aircraft, it can be dismantled for transportation simply by removing 13 quick-release pins.

41

VTOL Aircraft

The coming of helicopters satisfied some of the requirements of vertical take-off, but they were, and many still are, limited in their performance, with comparatively slow forward speeds, short range, and generally limited payload capacities. They lack the high forward speeds of conventional aircraft.

But even more than that, they are very expensive to operate.

During the 1920s and 1930s, experiments with VTOL (Vertical Take-off and Landing) aircraft were carried out in France, Britain, Germany and Spain, but these machines were much too heavy and complicated for practical use.

Lockheed XFV-1

Powered by an Allison T-40 turbo-prop engine of 5,850 hp, the Lockheed XFV-1 experimental VTOL fighter first flew in 1954. The four-point tail unit provided stability on the ground. Once airborne and in level flight, it could attain a speed of 500 mph.

Built in 1953, the Rolls-Royce Flying Bedstead was an experimental rig built to carry out VTOL tests. The thrust from two Nene turbo-jets was deflected downwards to provide lift off the ground. Stability in the air was maintained by two 'puffer' jets. Knowledge gained from tests with this rig paved the way for VTOL aircraft built in Britain.

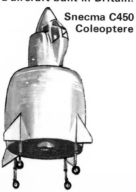

Snecma C450 Coleoptere

The French *Snecma C450 Coleoptere,* completed in 1958, was an experimental aircraft with no conventional wings. An 8,155-lb thrust *Atar* engine gave it its upward boost. After take-off, its barrel-shaped 'wing' provided the control surfaces.

The American Ryan X-13 Vertijet was another tail-sitter VTOL experimental aircraft. It could lift off from a combined launching ramp and servicing trolley. It first flew in 1957.

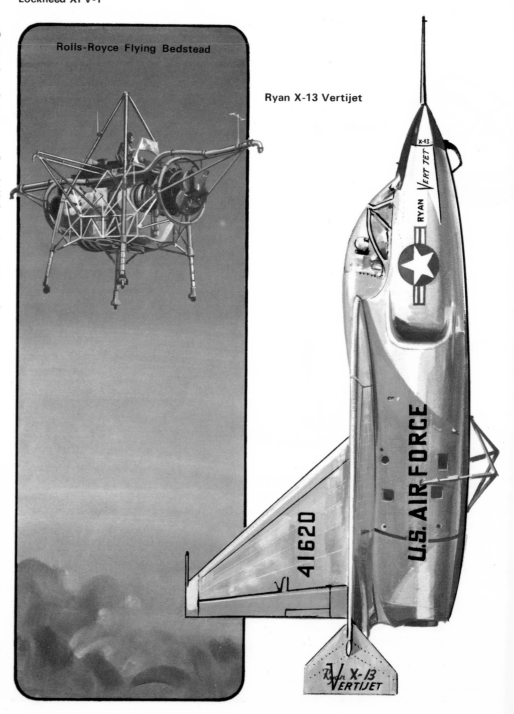

Rolls-Royce Flying Bedstead

Ryan X-13 Vertijet

Bell X-22-A

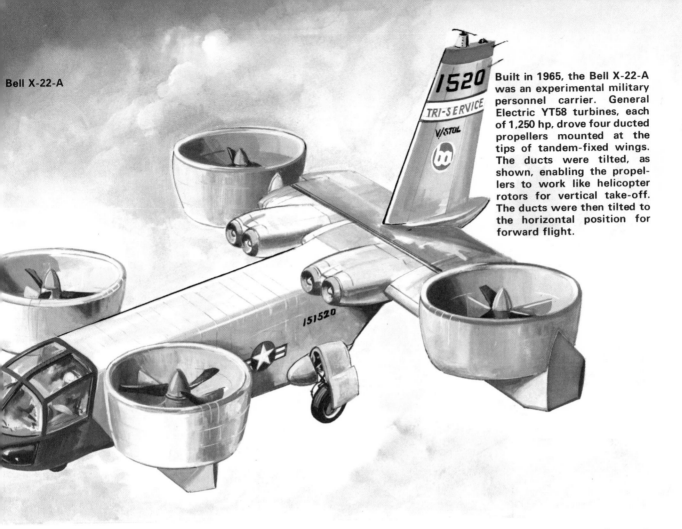

1520
TRI-SERVICE
V/STOL

151520

Built in 1965, the Bell X-22-A was an experimental military personnel carrier. General Electric YT58 turbines, each of 1,250 hp, drove four ducted propellers mounted at the tips of tandem-fixed wings. The ducts were tilted, as shown, enabling the propellers to work like helicopter rotors for vertical take-off. The ducts were then tilted to the horizontal position for forward flight.

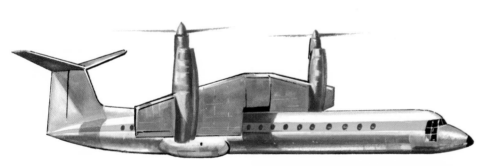

Among the many schemes in the pipe-line for VTOL airliners is this British Westland project — a tilt-wing aircraft. The day may come when airliners like this will replace the fixed-wing jet liners of today.

The Canadair CL-84 made its first flight in 1965. Another example of the tilt-wing system, it had additional twin rotor blades immediately behind the tail fin.

Engines powerful enough to lift them off the ground had not at that time been developed.

It was not until the 1950s, when jet and turbo-prop engines came into common use, that the first really practical, working VTOL aircraft came off the drawing board.

Designs varied from aircraft with wings that rotated, wings that tilted upwards for take-off, to tail-sitters, like the French *Coleoptere*.

VTOL aircraft form part of a new generation of aeroplanes, and it is likely that they will become the conventional aircraft of the very near future.

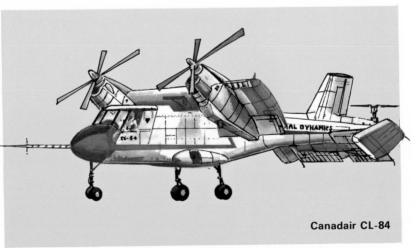

Canadair CL-84

Flying Oddities

One of the most remarkable 'airplanes' to come out of the Second World War was the Rotabuggy. It consisted of a standard army jeep with a special aerodynamic tail fin and rotor blades attached to the rear. The concept was revolutionary. The Rotabuggy could glide to the ground after release from an aircraft. Successful tests were carried out with them and they achieved speeds of up to 65 mph.

The air forces and commercial flying companies of the world abound with special purpose aircraft. These are aircraft which have been specially designed and built for a specific purpose, or perhaps aircraft which have been converted to carry out tasks which the production line model could not do.

Because of the very nature of these special duties, the resulting specially-built or adapted airplane often takes on a very odd appearance.

Airplane designers are masters of the art of improvisation, particularly in time of war. When massive airborne assaults were made against German-held areas during the Second World War, thousands of troops along with supporting equipment had to be dropped by parachute from the sky. Much of that equipment got damaged on impact, so the 'back-room boys' devised what

Grumman E-2A Hawkeye

The twin-engined Grumman E-24 Hawkeye, first flown in 1962, is a five-seat carrier-based early-warning detector aircraft. The huge 'saucer' above the fuselage houses sophisticated radar equipment for detecting enemy fighters on interception courses. Powered by two Allison turbo-prop engines, it has a flight endurance of seven hours.

The Australian Transavia PL-12 Airtruck is a multi-purpose aircraft. This one is equipped for seed- and fertilizer-spreading. Another version of the same aircraft can be used for passengers, cargo, as an ambulance, or for aerial survey.

Transavia PL-12 Airtruck

Lockheed Q-star

came to be known as the *Rotabuggy*, a jeep which could glide or fly to the ground from an aircraft.

Similarly, when the Germans infested the Allied shipping lanes with magnetic mines, British scientists found a method of detonating the mines from the air by converting *Wellington* bombers for the task.

Advances with special purpose air-craft continued to be made after the war. The carrier-borne *Hawkeye* early-warning aircraft is one. Another is the *Lockheed Q-star*, with its 'silent' engine. It can 'sneak' into enemy territory and carry out reconnaissance, without be-traying its presence by a noisy engine.

These, and a wide variety of less unusual looking aircraft, perform many odd but vital duties.

During the Second World War, magnetic mines proved a menace to Allied shipping, but the RAF found a way of combating them. Specially-adapted Wellington bombers, fitted with wide rings which produced a magnetic field, flew over the mines and ex-ploded them.

Wellington

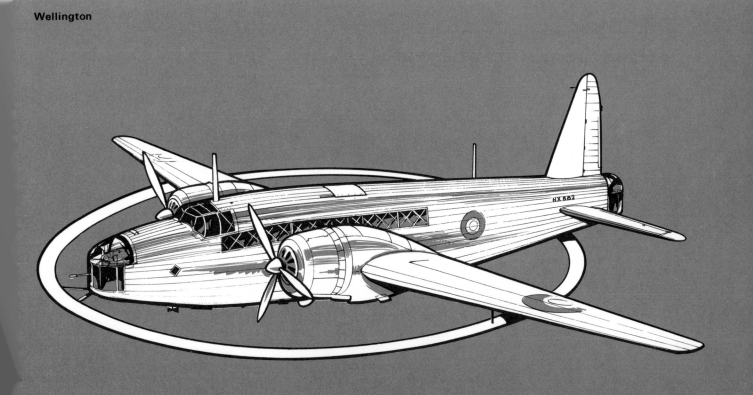

Experimental Aircraft

Ryan Flex-wing

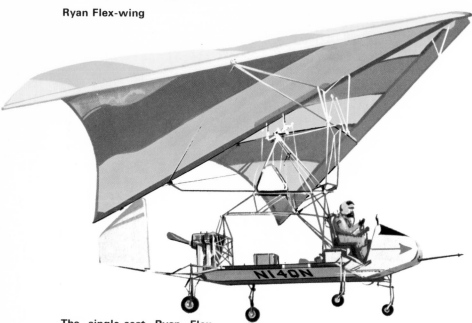

In recent years a succession of quite revolutionary experimental aircraft have been designed and flown; airplanes ranging in shape, size and speed from the small *Ryan Flex-wing* to the ultrasonic *Valkyrie*.

Created out of the imagination of designers whose experience ranges back over 70 years of powered flight, they are the prototypes and test beds for the aircraft of the future. From aircraft like these, and the experimental aircraft which came before them, man has acquired the technological skill which has enabled us to travel through space and land men on the moon.

Such a magnificent achievement could not have been possible without the pioneering spirit of the men who designed, built and flew airplanes like those we have seen in this book.

The single-seat Ryan Flex-wing is a purely experimental aircraft which was built to flight-test the V-shaped folding flexible nylon wing. The wing itself could be folded up quite easily when not in use.

The Douglas X-3 Stiletto was aptly named, with its elongated needle nose. Built in 1952 as a high-speed research aircraft, it was intended to fly at three times the speed of sound, but failed to achieve this high performance.

Douglas X-3 Stiletto

The North American XB-70 Valkyrie, first flown in 1964, is an enormous tail-first delta-wing aircraft. Originally designed as a bomber, it has changed to that of a mach 3 test aircraft.

The American Lockheed YF-12A has shattered world speed records, flying far in excess of three times the speed of sound.

North American XB-70 Valkyrie

Lockheed YF-12A

INDEX TO ILLUSTRATIONS